SAND & TRAFFIC

POEMS

PAULINE POWERS UCHMANOWICZ

CODHILL

CODHILL PRESS · NEW PALTZ · NEW YORK

THIS IS A CHAPBOOK
PUBLISHED BY CODHILL PRESS

This book is dedicated with loving gratitude to
Lawrence Uchmanowicz & Catherine Powers Uchmanowicz
in honor of their fiftieth anniversary.

ACKNOWLEDGMENTS

Grateful acknowledgement is made to editors of the publications
in which versions of the following poems first appeared or are forthcoming:
Chester Jones Foundation National Poetry Award Winners, 1985:
"For a Deaf Child's Sixth August"
Crazyhorse: "In the Passing Lane," "Pine Cone"
Free Lunch: "Wet Bathing Suit"
Greensboro Review: "The Motion"
Heliotrope: "Brush Burning"
Hunger Magazine: "Prophetess"
The Massachusetts Review: "Queen of the Pickpockets,"
"Visiting Rights," "Ideograph," "This Is Our World"
Mudfish: "Unmarried"
New American Writing: "Flowers, an Empty House and a Breakfast Roll"
Ohio Review: "Doing 'The Loop'"
Ploughshares: "*Explication de texte*"
Reading Objects 2002, Samuel Dorsky Museum of Art Exhibition Book:
"Woodstock Sculpture" (Lily Ente, 1905-1985, sculptor)
Southern Poetry Review: "the lower case"
Underwood Review: "Knee Deep in Mud My Mother,"
"Erroll Schneppor's Midnight Snack," "Love and Traffic"
Yet Another Small Magazine: "Tin Can Trout"
"Ideograph" was feature poem for April 17, 1998 on
David Lehman's *Poetry Daily* website, www.poems.com.

I also thank McDowell Colony, Yaddo, Hans Van de Bovenkamp Sculpture Garden,
Rock Cliff Poets, and New York State United University Professions.

ISBN 1-930337-16-7

Book design by Carla Rozman

Manufactured in the United States of America.
First Edition.

CONTENTS

THIS IS OUR WORLD

Scallop shells, hostages in my palms
I look to for guidance

on a softball field near a mesh fence
that my body cannot pass through, though

my shadow passes through its shadow.
Beyond a posted sign the moon

zippers through a thousand clouds
like sperm racing to ova,

like the red pupil in the iris of a fish
finning up a pool of goddesses.

At sea level
damp life jackets dangle

ornament style from the limbs of a tree.
Amphitrite's voice seeps from the foam:

Look everywhere,
you will find what you need.

WET BATHING SUIT

It reminds me of calendar time,
of a Harley Davidson beach towel
that just showed up during my youth
spent walking roughly two city blocks
from the house to the Heights
for swimming and transistors,
for diamond-oblivion Casino nights
when our neighborhood view of Martha's Vineyard
made squandering Cape Cod summer worthy.

Its clammy rub against my hazy
hot and humid half-life memory
summons the Moonwalk, Woodstock,
Chappaquiddick, nicks in my birth month
thirty years now as JFK Jr.'s plane
goes down and sinks west of the Sound.

Spreading thoughts of air and water
through my capillary system
the wet bathing suit I am seated in
touches me like my pilot father
or aviator brothers buzzing the yard
back and forth from Otis Air Base;
at apogee on the fabric its
drying illustration splashes me
with Dad in aqua-form,
treading the pool depths below me as
my first jump from a diving board flies.

TOURISTS

They will feast on bean and cod,
quick-waddle crosswalks with toddler

decoys toward coffee shop toilets
or lean mosquito-swollen arms clutching

road atlases out mini-van windows.
Tomorrow, sunrays now shielded by visors

from their eyes they will aim for,
spreading beach blankets as the *shush*

shush of waves rhyming at hide-tide mark
breaks riprap, wiping out damp squeals

surfacing deep from the lungs of tiny blondes
with sand toys digging, their grown-man

Red Sox cap-wearing fathers
exchanging jibes on behalf of the team,

together sliding—*safe*—the bases emotionally
familiar, so the world expands and shrinks.

Then should gray overcast July
afternoon roll through only to dissipate

("If you don't like the weather, just
wait a minute"), electric fans

stirring humidity with sea breezes,
we year-rounders will rise from naps,

gather round grills—swordfish and wine—
to speak of the old days

when THICKLY SETTLED signs meant
acre-lot neighborhoods, cranberry bog connecters

and farm stand pick-your-own corn.
Soon talk will turn to which barroom

ownership has changed hands,
who's living on a houseboat until August,

who made it big and who moved away
and who's back in town for another try

until names of the dead—by drugs,
booze, blood disease or drowning

(mercifully late or cruelly early)—again
pass among ourselves like lighted sparklers,

the sky's dippers replenishing its element
as sand turns cool beneath our feet.

FOR A DEAF CHILD'S SIXTH AUGUST

Noon on the porch in summer the woman
furled like pages of a magazine
after a day at the beach
has pulled her house plant out
of its original plastic nursery container
ready at last to transplant it
to a durable terra cotta and seen
just how pot bound it has become
with snarled roots strangling the nucleus
these last five years without her realizing,
her regret somewhat relieved in knowing
why it has not grown much.

So you see it may be merely rain rattling
over some morning kitchen distraction
or the kernel of doubt that the woman has tossed
like a grain of sand inside her
that makes her look up from the tan of her hands
packing down potting soil to suddenly
see how she nurtures a tangled spirit,
when your ears wrapped in corrective aids
struggle as the machinery clicks in place
and the door to your room seals you in.

BEACHSIDE BURIAL

Why finality,
beautiful middle child
full of leukemia,

splash a golden wave
may never roll back,
why we bury the young,

shovel in the dirt,
anthills
filling weedy cracks

in flagstone paths,
why butterflies
winking in a basket,

listening for
the book's closing,
hymn's amen,

ferry foghorn's
right-red-
returning

hosanna,
ashes to ashes,
sea to shining sea,

why no returns
for what was left
behind?

WOODSTOCK SCULPTURE

Night 8 the artist named
your onyx form,

reclined like a sphinx
at the beach.

Waves fold behind
your Belgian marble spine,

its smoothness worthy
of a Pharaoh.

How would you feel
buried neck-high in sand?

Where do I press my ear
to hear your heart of darkness?

SWIMMING HOLE

This is the world we waited for made new:
A rock beside Fourth Lake, kayaks

etching pencil-line wakes
below leafy banks where half-clad

divers on boulders appear
like early homo sapiens, paired

geese honking twice while we
tread water, still in the time

between made and unmade,
back-road shortcuts and mistletoe-

hemlock banter novel. I think:
Any moment you will lift

my fingertips to your lips,
loss and separation merging in

the brackish estuary of palm lines
joined as green eyes fix on brown.

But you resist like faces outlined
in the moon, mouths parted

starting a kiss yet forever apart.
Listen, I say. What is happening now:

This is your life. Hold it in your hands:
You will have no other life.

IDEOGRAPH

Edgy star, my acronical neighbor
leans from the ledge of her fifth-story roof

to fish the air with a rod and reel,
her line checked by a red chute,

a grammar school shaping her casting pool;
on a shore below

in a netted hat
another lures pet bees from combs,

the insects charmed by chugs of smoke,
stingers tempted, her hands ungloved:

as they hang in sync like a spell cast
by signaling semaphoric flags,

whiz means hook,
buzz honey, together waving.

KNEE DEEP IN MUD MY MOTHER

Would you be so terrifying
uncoffined, dried earth caked on your calves,
disintegrating in a field among weeds
like an animal whose death
makes a place large and strange?

Or, they could wait, they could
place us in one box,
carry us someplace pleasant
we have never visited and then
waking beside you in a strange city
I would be home.

THE MOTION

It tags the sky like moon gate or keyhole
just as I lean back in the tub,
blends through the red-gold leaves
and descends into the window sash,

a shirt tail tucking where the pane splits
two, this last gesture, then
the hot air balloon is lost to my flat skin

the way the horizontal hold finally controls
a television screen
so that even misplacing my buoyancy—

rising-hinge head lifting body—
like my sister missing two years
I do not recover where it hooks or lands.

VISITING RIGHTS

The father, inflating and releasing
        balloons
in diminishing size increments
        on Sunday,
seems to explain sex for his daughter,
        telling her

she will be less, then less, then less
        excited
by each projectile, and there is
        in the game
attraction, seduction and demise,
        ending finally

as she and her small, like herself
        small
cousin manage to burst them all and she
        goes crying
after one he discards in a car.
        Between the kids

there is a love affair that lasts
        the length
of the leaves' turning this year
        (green straight
to brown in one week with no bleeding),
        but with Dad

love is infectious, part mystery,
      part
ingenuousness, that simple, that
      three-year-old.
What they mold unplanned, is passed
      hand to hand,

like a plaster of Paris wedding bell,
      its casting
fondled, her cheek at Dad's bristles,
      her voice
ringing as then he whistles her back
      when she runs

unescorted for the road. Her play
      altered,
devotion faltering as her spry body
      wriggles
in his grasp, giving up, their limbs
      eloped.

DOING "THE LOOP"

Cold all day till five,
Corn born worthless in this state
Where the sun breaks
But finally for only
Five minutes or so
And I'm driving when its flat
Last line of light sinks red
Right at the edge
Of field piled field behind field

I lose the wheel to the mind
To the night to distraction—
Remember the future whole
Rooms carved marble
The world receiving you prime,
The past remote: *middle voice* in Greek,
An earthworm tracing the same path slow

This is where your soul belongs
Flat on concrete
Letting lights oval then blur,
Elongate white
Gates to New Zealand not visible by day

Next noon, same loop and the moon
Skywriting above a billboard sign:
I have learned to love this landscape,
And some day I'll just drive
Through the gates of the Lazy 'N,'
Tell the Iowa farmer
I like your land
Still green in November

BRUSH BURNING

Cows stand in their own footprints.
Snow crows mimic snow angels,

crunched torsos winging eastward
toward afternoon light.

So the country woman knows
to stir downed branches,

piled in her bonfire
like fallen crosses,

until the last twig dies. Then
the winter sky will blacken

as if witnessing the world's
reincarnation,

its longest night quickening
slickly as a slaughter blade.

PROPHETESS

I dream of births and deaths
"Confused cathedral," mother says

"If you dream of me don't tell me"
A horse in the room (that's panic)

Newborns stampede to my sleep
Lit by a toothed moon's shine

Buildings come to me just hours
Ahead of the wrecking ball

My teenage-suicide son's
Regular telegram arrives

He's just as tormented
On the other side

I see dust flats circling stars
Where planets form—a sign painted

These stairs reserved for pilgrims
Ascending on their knees

QUEEN OF THE PICKPOCKETS

I cannot remember all of their names
but I remember their cocks,
how each fit in my pocket like a nightstick
and acquired a life of its own,
then wrapped itself up like a warm revolver
to flee the scene of the crime,
with me wet on the bed in my nightshirt
as the door jerks shut
and a towel falls from the knob and I'm shook
and think some cat or cop has got in the room.
I do not remember the womb, being born or
those first invisible steps,
why I could not eat asparagus (they smell like
penis, like work) or sleep with beige men.
Streetwalking is like wearing stripped cellophane
or glass—why ask about bread
or what the motivation is?
People are always trying to track down how
I got sidetracked, like the detective
who nearly mowed me once over, spotted me
at a nightspot but tractors don't distract me,
I notice things, a man comes and there's something
funny about his shoes, black and shiny—
you can always tell a dick by his shoes.
But did this dick's dick fit me like a gumshoe
then need a shoehorn to pry itself out?
He was horny but I wouldn't touch a fin of his money
or talk pillow, I talked skywriting and wished on a
star; it turned out to be an airplane.
Dorothy fell in a tornado and she was in a balloon
on the way home; she was plodding, I am plotting
potting two sets of sheets under a nightshade

and I would take a Tinted Man even if what stinks
about being a person like a car is there are so many
parts: my tongue becomes irritated when overworked
like two black tennis balls straddling a rusted can
doing time on the roof.
I could quit climbing the walls if I wanted
as aloof as the Dance of the Question Marks.
I got no schedule—this whole town's for sale.
I could pop off your pants, bake a dummy, shake your
bag of bones, romance the stone in the alley and shout:
"Hey baby eat my house!"
and steal your whole house if you let me in,
but it's no reason to expect something to eat.
Nowadays what really takes my head off is a soft moon.
To the man crouched under a stairwell flipping a stone
I tell, "You have a nice crotch, let's arrest ourselves.
We are both brothers. We are both sisters.
We are both antelope with teeth of grass."

ERROLL SCHNEPPOR'S MIDNIGHT SNACK

I know I'm late—someone was trying to make me obey the speed limit.
I looked for a parking space for six months.
Funny thing, that car, so big it can't fit inside me but it's mine.
It's the biggest thing I own.
This taco looks like twenty miles of bad road.
I wonder what Milicent is doing.
When we met it was like seeing the pick-a-card trick for the first time.
After a while it was like watching a test pattern.
Guess all we ever had in common was warts.
Once she took me to a movie—through the whole thing
I was nervous my foot would fall asleep and I'd get up and fall.
Nobody'd get blown away in my movie.
There's someone over there with one of those portable phones.
Milicent says don't ever let anyone in your house who's wearing one of those.
If they're carrying a phone booth on their back, okay.
The first time I asked for her phone number she told me:
Look it up in the dictionary.
A dart tossed is a dart lost—no rethrows.
I'm already mixed but I'm shoutin' for the next round.
Once Milicent ordered an "Alcatraz"—water with a lemon peel.
She used to be afraid of dying.
But one morning me and Millie stopped at Grand Slam Liquors for a six pack.
Later we pulled off the road into a cemetery to piss.
Warm sun behind a mausoleum made us wanna stay there forever.
All we really have is our ignorance.
I got a good lookout on life.
Let's finish these and go throw Millie in the pool.

TIN CAN TROUT

Drinking, I begin to miss you
Our empty breakfast glasses
Still around the chess board

Only this morning you confessed
The toothbrush we shared for months
Never belonged to you

FLOWERS, AN EMPTY HOUSE AND A BREAKFAST ROLL

Winging an equator along its mid-wall
this room patterns a fascination with ducks
in perpetual flight—this is how

I would like you to endure, even now,
as down the street from this neighbor's house
the empty space you've left wanders its spirit

like a busload of ballerinas. Last week
a plastic dinosaur the size of a cat
sat on a child's front porch, the best toy ever,

on the car radio Japanese jazz and the sylvan sun
glistened the cloaks of grazing cows.
Let us call time an activist.

Let it be always the day they call off politics,
the day three bodies form a straight line.
Let time be tender and sink in,

like a cluster of friends viewed through a lit
doorway, like baseball on TV, so airy
and clean. Let the fireflies out—cling

clang train. A garage band will play in a barn
while outside, unless for the sake of spring,
there is no good reason for the bonfire.

EXPLICATION DE TEXTE

Natives rubbing sticks spark the first line
only to canoe straight out of the stanza,
usurped by leaves cackling under a magnifying glass

followed in the next tercet by a distilled lesson
on the invention of matches: phosphorous discovered
1680; strike books manufactured 1889;

and just when you count yourself a third-through
captive, blindfolded in the pitch of typeset,
a firing squad shouldering muskets forms

a column of dropped knees, shots got off
at the heart of discourse answered by caesura,
tripping an enjambment chain

reaction further up the poem when, presaged by altar
candles casting apse shadows, campers flicker flash-
lights skyward towards the dangling Milky Way's

dying luminosity, making way for the turn, where
some disgruntled peasant tosses a matchstick into
a powder keg, the verse's fuse fizzles down and

time bomb detonates, its epiphany dynamited
to smithereens by penultimate fireworks as
a scout deciphers grand finale smoke signals.

the lower case

it's visceral the way the g
of green or ground

dips below the sentence line
planting cabbage in a child

naked to the waist
seated before a bowl of borscht

purpling herself with a spoon
turned sideways

as brain gears crank
in ukrainian and english—

muse or lucky ear—
whatever her secret may she

never in any language
suffer from onomatophobia

or fear stars calling fields miracles
whether or not we name them

UNMARRIED

I prefer to study stars and yet
in a living room chair I sit
and wonder what a static television
skyline can tell me about night illumination.
Since I am not called to act
to escape into that screen's city seems safe,
for in truth, my ache: it is not theatrical.
In real-life scenes I exit obligations
not of my own invention.
Hazy from the TV's low grade din of dots
I shut my eyes to blackness and see
a family situation, satellite commitment,
and from my womb a new planet
and another, another.

PINE CONE

Pine cone on my fire escape, you sir,
giant rake-of-a-seed, need one day claim
to be extinct, so long as my genus keeps up
saluting uniforms enough to insure
each of your shingles cups a yarmulke of dust
over the plan of human to scrap the soul of human,
if tilted to scatter like shards from a grenade
flung from the manicured corporate hand
of an accountant who debits your future kin
to advertising expenses. Mute fruit, you all
of all that stood alone before mortar shrunk
stars, the sky stolen in shades of ambush,
if a viper shakes your spiny claws,
give thanks, thanks! for the dancing lesson!

BLACK ANGEL

Felderverth Family Monument

A graveside place for trysts,
what we wanted was
her stark opposite:

wingspans
steely as Brooklyn Bridge,
lyrical as Hermes',

us a pair of hawks
teaching our baby
bird to fly,

hearts lifting
above those marble
eyes said to curse,

underground
a buried lover's tale
long done

while ours still fledgling,
its objective
correlative

obscured like her
obsidian shadow
against night,

statue oblivious
to everlasting
utterance.

LOVE AND TRAFFIC

If a flag at half-mast meant someone loved you,
salt swilled in a drop of wine
did not resemble a pregnancy test,
a dictionary diagram of vocal cords
looked other than like a vagina
("open" on voice "closed" on whisper),
to give with condition meant less
than to take or birthrates could be ignored,

then we would love as ideally as driving 33
MPH through Manhattan and never hitting a red light,
forgetting how we move in traffic, alone yet
communal like cows grazing hillsides
ahead where a toll road ends us,
one right, one left of our pledges of allegiance.

IN THE PASSING LANE

The you inside of me today seems tangible.
A clapboard cottage beside a frozen pond: that is you.
My drive up the road: that is you too.
Like reading a sign, I see in the distance called past
you passing me the concept of constantly holding
friends in my mind, which reaffirms that all time
happens at once, as firmly as these pines line
the side of the road. In this moment, as a line of slow-
moving cars with headlights on in daylight
moves on the other side of the median strip,
I recollect last week, in the face of a youth
bound for Alaska, you, red-headed parrot of travel
set against gimmicks that make us hate the cold.
This is told to you in this and every other moment.